KU-713-770

Personal, Learning & Thinking Skills in PSHE

Self-Managers

Eileen Osborne
& Steph Yates

LIVERPOOL JMU LIBRARY

3 1111 01383 4609

Folens

© 2009 Folens Limited, on behalf of the authors.

United Kingdom: Folens Publishers, Waterslade House, Thame Road, Haddenham, Buckinghamshire, HP17 8NT.
Email: folens@folens.com Website: www.folens.com

Ireland: Folens Publishers, Greenhills Road, Tallaght, Dublin 24.
Email: info@folens.ie Website: www.folens.ie

Folens publications are protected by international copyright laws. All rights are reserved. The copyright of all materials in this publication, except where otherwise stated, remains the property of the publisher and the authors. No part of this publication may be reproduced, stored in a retrieval system, or transmitted, in any form or by any means, for whatever purpose, without the written permission of Folens Limited except where authorized.

Folens allows photocopying of pages marked 'copiable page' for educational use, providing that this use is within the confines of the purchasing institution. Copiable pages should not be declared in any return in respect of any photocopying licence.

Eileen Osborne and Steph Yates hereby assert their moral rights to be identified as the authors of this work in accordance with the Copyright, Designs and Patents Act 1988.

Editor: Louise Clark
Series designer and layout: Fiona Webb
Illustrations: **Catherine Ward:** 14, 21, 22, 24, 38, 44, 48, 50, 51, 62; **Sarah Wimperis of GCI:** 26 (top left and right, bottom right), 27, 64; **Bridget Dowty of GCI:** 26 (bottom left), 43.
Cover design: Form (www.form.uk.com)

The websites recommended in this publication were correct at the time of going to press, however websites may have been removed or web addresses changed since that time. Folens has made every attempt to suggest websites that are reliable and appropriate for student's use. It is not unknown for unscrupulous individuals to put unsuitable material on websites that may be accessed by students. Teachers should check all websites before allowing students to access them. Folens is not responsible for the content of external websites.

For general spellings Folens adheres to *Oxford Dictionary of English*, Second Edition (Revised), 2005.

First published 2009 by Folens Limited.

Every effort has been made to contact copyright holders of material used in this publication. If any copyright holder has been overlooked, we will be pleased to make any necessary arrangements.

British Library Cataloguing in Publication Data. A catalogue record for this publication is available from the British Library.

ISBN 978-1-85008-453-2   Folens code FD4532

Contents

Self-Managers

'The personal, learning and thinking skills (PLTS) framework supports young people in their learning across the curriculum. The skills should be developed through a range of experiences and subject contexts.'

(QCA)

This series, PLTS in PSHE, uses the PLTS framework as a linking bridge to the PSHE programmes of study. It provides a context for PSHE departments to contribute to the overall PLTS skills and competencies, and in doing so provides students with the ability to transfer what they have learnt in PSHE across other curriculum areas.

This is one of six books in the series and each book links to one of the six groups of skills in the PLTS framework. This book has as its focus 'self-managers'.

SELF-MANAGERS

Focus

Young people organise themselves, showing personal responsibility, initiative, creativity and enterprise with a commitment to learning and self-improvement. They actively embrace change, responding positively to new priorities, coping with challenges and looking for opportunities.

Skills, behaviours and personal qualities

Young people:
◎ seek out challenges or new responsibilities and show flexibility when priorities change
◎ work towards goals, showing initiative, commitment and perseverance
◎ organise time and resources, prioritising actions
◎ anticipate, take and manage risks
◎ deal with competing pressures, including personal and work-related demands
◎ respond positively to change, seeking advice and support when needed
◎ manage their emotions, and build and maintain relationships.

© Qualifications and Curriculum Authority

Throughout the book students are encouraged to organise themselves in various ways and show personal responsibility while coping with change and challenge. They actively pursue new opportunities and areas for self-improvement. One important aspect of *Self-Managers* is that students learn to manage their emotions and build relationships within the general framework of becoming 'self-managers'. This book is divided into units for Key Stage 3 and Key Stage 4.

Teacher's notes

Each unit has accompanying Teacher's Notes which give information on the unit, and ideas on how to use the Activity sheets, starters and plenaries. Each unit has its own set of objectives set out in the Teacher's Notes.

Assessment/Progress sheets

On pages 6–7 there are two sheets which focus on student progress and learning. The two sheets can be used to assess progress, decide on targets and help students to move to a higher level in their learning.

	Unit 1: Review and planning	Unit 2: Be enterprising!	Unit 3: Emotional wellbeing	Unit 4: Exploring feelings	Unit 5: Grandparents	Unit 6: The same but different	Unit 7: No Make-up Day	Unit 8: The centre of attention	Unit 9: Not quite a 'dragons' den!	Unit 10: Where else?
PSHE Programmes of Study for England	Personal wellbeing: 1.1 Personal identities; 1.2 Healthy lifestyles; 1.3 Risk; 1.4 Relationships Economic wellbeing and financial capability: 1.1 Career	Personal wellbeing: 1.1 Personal identities; 1.3 Risk; 1.4 Relationships Economic wellbeing and financial capability: 1.2 Capability; 1.3 Risk	Personal wellbeing: 1.1 Personal identities; 1.3 Risk; 1.4 Relationships	Personal wellbeing: 1.1 Personal identities; 1.2 Healthy lifestyles; 1.3 Risk; 1.4 Relationships	Personal wellbeing: 1.1 Personal identities; 1.2 Healthy lifestyles; 1.3 Risk; 1.4 Relationships; 1.5 Diversity	Personal wellbeing: 1.1 Personal identities; 1.3 Risk; 1.4 Relationships; 1.5 Diversity Economic wellbeing and financial capability: 1.2 Capability; 1.3 Risk	Personal wellbeing: 1.1 Personal identities; 1.2 Healthy lifestyles; 1.3 Risk; 1.4 Relationships	Personal wellbeing: 1.1 Personal identities; 1.2 Healthy lifestyles; 1.3 Risk; 1.4 Relationships	Personal wellbeing: 1.1 Personal identities; 1.3 Risk; 1.4 Relationships; 1.5 Diversity Economic wellbeing and financial capability: 1.2 Capability; 1.3 Risk	Personal wellbeing: 1.1 Personal identities; 1.3 Risk; 1.4 Relationships
Curriculum for Excellence for Scotland	Health and wellbeing: Mental, emotional, social and physical wellbeing; Planning for choices and changes	Health and wellbeing: Mental, emotional, social and physical wellbeing	Health and wellbeing: Mental, emotional, social and physical wellbeing	Health and wellbeing: Mental, emotional, social and physical wellbeing	Health and wellbeing: Mental, emotional, social and physical wellbeing; Relationships, sexual health and parenthood	Health and wellbeing: Mental, emotional, social and physical wellbeing	Health and wellbeing: Mental, emotional, social and physical wellbeing	Health and wellbeing: Mental, emotional, social and physical wellbeing	Health and wellbeing: Mental, emotional, social and physical wellbeing	Health and wellbeing: Mental, emotional, social and physical wellbeing
Personal and Social Education Framework for Wales	Active citizenship; Health and emotional wellbeing; Moral and spiritual development; Preparing for lifelong learning	Active citizenship; Health and emotional wellbeing; Moral and spiritual development	Health and emotional wellbeing; Moral and spiritual development	Active citizenship; Health and emotional wellbeing; Moral and spiritual development	Active citizenship; Health and emotional wellbeing; Moral and spiritual development	Active citizenship; Health and emotional wellbeing; Moral and spiritual development	Active citizenship; Health and emotional wellbeing; Moral and spiritual development	Active citizenship; Health and emotional wellbeing; Moral and spiritual development	Active citizenship; Health and emotional wellbeing; Moral and spiritual development	Health and emotional wellbeing; Preparing for lifelong learning
Revised Curriculum for Northern Ireland: Learning for Life and Work	Learning for life and work: Personal understanding; Mutual understanding; Citizenship; Employability	Learning for life and work: Personal understanding; Mutual understanding; Moral character; Economic awareness; Citizenship	Learning for life and work: Personal understanding; Mutual understanding; Moral character; Cultural understanding	Learning for life and work: Personal understanding; Mutual understanding; Moral character	Learning for life and work: Personal understanding; Mutual understanding; Moral character; Citizenship	Learning for life and work: Personal understanding; Mutual understanding; Citizenship	Learning for life and work: Personal understanding; Mutual understanding; Citizenship	Learning for life and work: Personal understanding; Mutual understanding	Learning for life and work: Personal understanding; Mutual understanding; Moral character	Learning for life and work: Personal understanding
Every Child Matters	Enjoy and achieve; Make a positive contribution	Be healthy; Stay safe	Stay safe; Make a positive contribution	Enjoy and achieve; Make a positive contribution	Enjoy and achieve; Make a positive contribution	Be healthy; Stay safe	Stay safe; Make a positive contribution	Enjoy and achieve; Make a positive contribution	Make a positive contribution; Achieve economic wellbeing	Enjoy and achieve
Social and Emotional Aspects of Learning	Social skills: Self awareness; Motivation	Social skills: Self awareness; Motivation	Social skills: Self awareness; Motivation	Social skills: Self awareness; Motivation	Social skills: Self awareness; Motivation	Social skills: Self awareness; Motivation	Social skills: Self awareness; Motivation	Social skills: Self awareness; Motivation	Social skills:: Self awareness; Motivation	Social skills: Self awareness; Motivation

LIVERPOOL JOHN MOORES UNIVERSITY LEARNING SERVICES

Self-Managers

Tick the box to show what applies to you at the start of the unit and then again at the end.

I can...

	At the start of this unit			At the end of this unit		
	🙂	😐	☹️	🙂	😐	☹️
◎ look for challenges or new responsibilities						
◎ show flexibility when priorities change						
◎ work towards goals						
◎ show initiative, commitment and perseverance						
◎ organise my time and resources						
◎ prioritise what I need to do						
◎ anticipate, take and manage risks						
◎ deal with pressures of all kinds						
◎ respond positively to change, seeking advice and support when needed						
◎ manage my emotions, and build and maintain relationships						

My targets at the end of this unit are:

1 _____

_____

2 _____

_____

3 _____

_____

PLTS in PSHE: Self-Managers   © Folens (copiable page)

Self-Managers

You have now assessed how effective a self-manager you are. This sheet is for you to see how you can progress and improve in the skills needed to be a self-manager. Each statement indicates what you should do to move to being a good or an excellent self-manager.

◎ **I look for challenges or new responsibilities.**
I must actively look for new challenges or responsibilities.
I must accept that these will have an effect on my time and life.

◎ **I can show flexibility when priorities change.**
I must make sure I understand what it means to be flexible.
I must accept that there may be times when priorities will change.

◎ **I can work towards goals.**
I must understand what a goal is and why they are a necessary part of life.
I must learn to accept that some goals are short term and others are long term.

◎ **I can show initiative, commitment and perseverance.**
I must understand that initiative is sometimes threatening to people.
I must understand that commitment and perseverance take time and effort.

◎ **I can organise my time and resources and prioritise what I need to do.**
I must understand that I need to be organised if I am to fully succeed.
I must have confidence in my ability to prioritise.

◎ **I can anticipate, take and manage risks.**
I must understand that risk is part of being a successful self-manager.
I must learn never to be afraid of anticipating the next step/steps and acting accordingly.

◎ **I can deal with pressure of all kinds.**
I must understand that there are always pressures in life.
I must learn to cope with those pressures.

◎ **I can respond positively to change.**
I must accept that change is part of life.
I must learn to accept change in a positive and formative way.

◎ **I can seek advice and support when it is needed.**
I must never be afraid to look for advice or support when I need to.
I must accept that asking for advice or support is not a sign of weakness.

◎ **I can manage my emotions, and build and maintain relationships.**
I must learn how to manage my emotions.
I must accept that relationships have to be worked at.

© Folens (copiable page)

Objectives

By the end of the lesson, students will:

◎ have understood what short term and long term planning means.

◎ have identified why and how they can manage their own time and resources.

◎ have shown that they can respond to the pressures placed upon them by personal and work-related demands.

Prior knowledge

None.

Links

Personal, Social, Health and Economic Education Programmes of Study for England: Personal wellbeing: 1.1 Personal identities; 1.2 Healthy lifestyles; 1.3 Risk; 1.4 Relationships. Economic wellbeing and financial capability: 1.1 Career.

Curriculum for Excellence for Scotland: Health and Wellbeing: Health and wellbeing: Mental, emotional, social and physical wellbeing; Planning for choices and changes.

Personal and Social Education Framework for Wales: Active citizenship; Health and emotional wellbeing; Moral and spiritual development; Preparing for lifelong learning.

Revised Curriculum for Northern Ireland: Learning for Life and Work: Personal understanding; Mutual understanding; Citizenship; Employability.

Background

Students have for many years been encouraged to understand themselves and to set targets and goals. Within the framework of PLTS the six groups of skills have promoted self-examination and determination. In this unit students are encouraged to work towards goals and in doing so they will fulfil the demands of the concept of self-management. This unit therefore serves to expand the concept and allows students to gain a greater understanding of their own needs and possibilities as 'self-managers'.

Starter activity

Begin with a general discussion about why individuals set targets and goals, the purpose of them and how students might benefit if they commit to chosen goals and persevere with them. You could think about some well-known people, for example sports men or women, and consider what their goals/targets have been in the past.

Activity sheets

Activity sheet **1.1 The Termly Review (1)** encourages students to focus on their work and behaviour in one term. This generic sheet can be used at the end of each term if wished. Students should work alone and think carefully about each statement before recording their answers. Comments and examples will help to open up and clarify the answers. A full discussion of the answers should follow. Before the lesson the teacher should complete a copy of Activity sheet **1.2 The Termly Review (2)** for each student. Students should be given their named sheet after they have completed Activity sheet **1.1 The Termly Review (1)** and should compare and contrast what has been said.

Activity sheet **1.3 Short/Long Term Plans** should be used with Activity sheets **1.1** and **1.2**. Students are asked to look at what their short term and long term plans should be in the light of the results from these previous sheets. They should focus on what they need to do in order to succeed or be even more successful.

Activity sheet **1.4 Making It Work** allows students to consider how well they anticipate and deal with pressure by giving them five scenarios to read and then respond to. This could be extended by asking students to write a further two scenarios and then giving them to a partner to answer.

Plenary

Students should work in pairs to discuss what this unit has taught them about themselves and their ability to plan and work towards goals.

1.1 The Termly Review (1)

How have you worked and behaved this term? How have you responded to necessary changes? Have you met the goals that you set yourself or that your teachers set you?

This sheet will help you think about all these things and then record your progress. Be honest about how things have gone! Record a score from 1–5 for each statement:
1 = Totally disagree; 2 = Disagree; 3 = Neither agree nor disagree; 4 = Agree;
5 = Totally agree. If there is any statement which does not apply to you write
N/A instead of a number. Use the last column to add examples to support your scores.

Statement	1–5	Your comments and examples
I have worked as hard as I can in all my subjects		
I have behaved as well as I can in all my subjects		
I have completed all my homework to the best of my ability		
I have met any/all targets given to me		
I have responded to change when told to do so		
I have managed my time well both in school and at home for homework		
I have shown commitment and perseverance in all my work		
I can prioritise work to be done		

1.2 The Termly Review (2)

This sheet has been completed by your teacher. Compare the answers below with your answers from Activity sheet 1.1. Discuss with a partner the similarities and differences between the two sheets and what you intend to do if there are any major differences.

Student's Name: _____

Your teacher has recorded a number 1–5 for each statement below: 1 = Totally disagree; 2 = Disagree; 3 = Neither agree nor disagree; 4 = Agree; 5= Totally agree.

If there is any statement which does not apply, your teacher has written N/A instead of a number.

Statement	1–5	Teacher's comments and examples
Worked as hard as possible in all subjects		
Behaved as well as possible in all subjects		
Completed all homework to the best of their ability		
Met any/all targets given		
Responded to change when told to do so		
Managed time well both in school and at home for homework		
Showed commitment and perseverance in all their work		
Prioritised work to be done		

PLTS in PSHE: Self-Managers

© Folens (copiable page)

1.3 Short/Long Term Plans

You will need Activity sheets 1.1 and 1.2 to use with this sheet.

This sheet enables you to decide on your short/long term plans, your plans for next term and beyond, so that you will make progress or succeed in areas you may never have thought about before. Remember to be totally honest when you fill this sheet in!

MY PLANNING SHEET

Statement	Planning (action I will take)
I will look for challenges/ new responsibilities	
I will work towards my goals and not give up	
I will organise my time well – both in school and at home for homework	
I will prioritise my work	
I will deal with pressure as needed	
I will look for advice/help when I need it	
I will take full responsibility for my work and my actions	
I will commit myself to learning as much as I can	

1.4 Making It Work

Can you anticipate, i.e. think ahead, take and manage risks?

Can you deal with pressures, including personal
and work-related demands?

People who succeed are the ones who can anticipate and deal with pressures. How effective are you in these two areas? Be honest when you answer the questions below!

You have been given an English project for homework. You have four weeks in which to complete it and hand it in. What do you do?	
Your RE teacher has given you a group project to do. You have been asked to present it in a 'different and inventive way'. What would you do? Are you prepared to take risks with the presentation? How?	
You have four extensive pieces of work due in within two days of each other. How do you manage the pressure of this?	
Family worries and problems are beginning to affect your school work. What do you do? Who do you go to for help and advice?	
Your parents have booked a holiday during your school exam time. You are told by your Year Leader that if you go it will go on your record as truancy as the time off will not be authorised. What do you do? What is most important to you?	

PLTS in PSHE: Self-Managers

© Folens (copiable page)

Objectives

By the end of the lesson, students will:

◎ have identified a new challenge and shown flexibility in their approach to it.

◎ have understood the need to work towards goals, managing time and resources when doing this.

◎ have shown that they can respond positively to change.

Prior knowledge

None.

Links

Personal, Social, Health and Economic Education Programmes of Study for England: Personal wellbeing: 1.1 Personal identities; 1.3 Risk; 1.4 Relationships. Economic wellbeing and financial capability: 1.2 Capability; 1.3 Risk.

Curriculum for Excellence for Scotland: Health and Wellbeing: Health and wellbeing: Mental, emotional, social and physical wellbeing.

Personal and Social Education Framework for Wales: Active citizenship; Health and emotional wellbeing; Moral and spiritual development.

Revised Curriculum for Northern Ireland: Learning for Life and Work: Personal understanding; Mutual understanding; Moral character; Economic awareness; Citizenship.

Background

The concept of 'active citizenship' is now well embedded in our educational system. The social, cultural, moral and spiritual aspects of the curriculum are also firmly in place. This unit adds those areas to PSHE in order to allow students to approach their work in a truly cross curricular way while at the same time fulfilling the 'self-managers' area of PLTS. Students are encouraged to think for themselves while at the same time being part of a team. They are also encouraged to take full responsibility for all parts of their work. This unit could take two or three lessons to complete.

Starter activity

Start a general discussion about the local area and some of the problems there may be. It would be helpful to have some newspaper articles if any are available, or you could do some prior research about what local people think the problems are – without giving students too many ideas for their work!

Activity sheets

Activity sheet **2.1 The Problem (1)** focuses on a group of young people who are discussing the problems in their local area. Read through this sheet with students. Compare and contrast the problems here with those you discussed in the starter activity.

Using Activity sheets **2.1 The Problem (1)** and **2.2 The Problem (2)** students should work in small groups to decide on what they think are the top four problems in their local area and examine the effects those problems have had or are having on the area. They should then decide which of the four problems is the biggest.

Activity sheet **2.3 Teamwork (1)** allows students to move away temporarily from the problem-solving work to look in detail at the strengths of those in their group and decide which role each individual will play in the forthcoming activity. Students should be given Activity sheet **2.4 The Solution (1)** so that they can direct their discussions accordingly.

Activity sheet **2.4** needs careful and thoughtful discussion before students reach agreement as to what could be done. Likewise their ideas about adapting the solution should be thought through carefully: what if they could only carry out part of their solution? What part would they choose to focus on?

Activity sheet **2.5 The Solution (2)** asks students to present their findings to adults and in so doing show perseverance and commitment to their work. This could be a second or even third lesson for this unit and students should be encouraged to plan their presentation in a creative and enterprising manner.

Plenary

Discuss with students what they as a class have learned from this activity and look at how they as individuals have risen to the challenges they faced.

2.1 The Problem (1)

Baz, Will, Emma and Nadia have looked at their local community and come up with a list of what they think are the top five problems. Read what they say.

Litter is a big problem. The place looks really dirty and the litter is everywhere. Nobody uses the litter bins, they just throw stuff on the floor. It blows all over.

I think the biggest problem is that we have nowhere to go in the evening and we just hang around. That's when trouble starts and people ring the Police.

What about the lack of a play area for the kids? They play on the streets and could have an accident. The old play area was rubbish but at least it was there. Since the council got rid of it there's nothing.

A lot of people around here have lost their jobs and haven't got a lot of money to spend. That's a problem for us all isn't it? Those people feel as if nobody cares about them.

But there's nowhere for elderly people either! They must get fed up being in the house all the time and should be able to meet up with their mates, somewhere warm and friendly where they can chat and have a meal.

PLTS in PSHE: Self-Managers © Folens (copiable page)

2.2 The Problem (2)

You will need Activity sheet 2.1 to use with this Activity sheet. Your task is to work in small groups and decide on what you think are the top four problems in your community or local area. For each problem you should say what effect it has on the people in your area. Once you have decided you should then decide which of your four problems is your 'Number 1', i.e. the one that you think is the biggest problem, the one you would most like to do something about.

	Problem	Effect on local area
1		
2		
3		
4		

We have decided that the biggest problem is number _____.

2.3 Teamwork

Your task here is to list the members of your team, say what their strengths are and what roles each member of the team would be willing to play in the activity you will be doing next – finding a solution to your Number 1 problem!

Name	Strengths	Role(s)

 © Folens (copiable page)

2.4 The Solution (1)

Use this sheet to work out a solution to your Number 1 problem.

Our biggest local problem is:

This is a problem because:

This is what we think could be done about the problem:

If necessary we could adapt our ideas by:

2.5 The Solution (2)

As a group you need to 'sell' your solution to your Headteacher and/or members of the local council or community. You should use this page to plan your approach and presentation. Use the headings given.

As a community we need to solve this problem because:

The short/long term benefits for the community would be:

We think the following individuals/groups would help in this project:

Our suggested name and/or symbol for this project would be:

PLTS in PSHE: Self-Managers © Folens (copiable page)

Teacher's Notes

Objectives

By the end of the lesson, students will:

◎ have identified whether or not they are emotionally literate.

◎ understand when to seek advice/support and have identified who to go to for this.

◎ understand what a 'challenge' is and how to plan for these.

Prior knowledge

None.

Links

Personal, Social, Health and Economic Education Programmes of Study for England: Personal wellbeing: 1.1 Personal identities; 1.3 Risk; 1.4 Relationships.

Curriculum for Excellence for Scotland: Health and Wellbeing: Health and wellbeing: Mental, emotional, social and physical wellbeing.

Personal and Social Education Framework for Wales: Health and emotional wellbeing; Moral and spiritual development.

Revised Curriculum for Northern Ireland: Learning for Life and Work: Personal understanding; Mutual understanding; Moral character; Cultural understanding.

Background

SEAL (Social and emotional aspects of learning) and PLTS (Personal, learning and thinking skills) have brought the area of emotional wellbeing (emotional literacy) to the forefront of educational debate and practice yet again. This unit enables students to explore this area for themselves.

Starter activity

Ask students to give examples of how they react in various situations. For example what do they do if someone calls them names? Are there occasions when they very easily or quickly get angry? Do they often feel very happy/unhappy? Discuss these reactions and feelings.

Activity sheets

Allow students to complete Activity sheet **3.1 Emotional Literacy** on their own without

discussing it at all. When completed they should add up the number of A/S/N answers given. A majority of As would indicate a high level of emotional literacy, a high level of Ns would indicate the opposite. Most students will fall somewhere in the middle, and will probably have more S answers. Discuss their responses and talk about what they have learned about themselves from this quiz.

Activity sheet **3.2 Who Can I Talk To?** should also be completed individually and then discussed afterwards. It would be interesting to compare students' lists and then construct a final list of the top five people students in the class would talk to. This sheet encourages students to consider who to go to when they need help/advice and reinforces the advice given in Unit 4 'Exploring feelings'. These two units could be used together as one larger unit covering two lessons.

Activity sheet **3.3 Ways Of Opening Up** allows students to examine how two young people open up and deal with emotions and pressure. Students should then write down how they deal with pressures and emotions. This should be followed up by a class discussion on this with volunteers giving their points of view.

Activity sheet **3.4 Can We Help?** gives students the real life example of a group of Year 8 students who designed a challenge for Year 7 students. After reading the article, students should work in small groups to answer the questions given.

Activity sheet **3.5 Being A Mentor** is again taken from real life and focuses on students seeking out challenges and new responsibilities, taking the initiative and being enterprising. In answering the questions they bring the focus of the work completed in the unit back to emotional literacy/ wellbeing and the work can therefore be used as a review of the work in the unit.

Plenary

Discuss with students what they as a group could do in school to help others to become more emotionally literate.

3.1 Emotional Literacy

Emotional literacy:
The ability to manage yourself and your own emotions
and to understand the feelings and emotions of others.

Take the quiz below to find out whether or not you are emotionally literate.
For each statement you should tick the appropriate box:
A = Always, S = Sometimes, N = Never.

Statement	A	S	N
When you are wrong can you admit it?			
Can you talk to other people about how you are feeling?			
Can you tell what someone else is feeling, e.g. when they are angry, happy or sad?			
Do you know your own moods, e.g. can you tell when you are angry, happy or sad?			
Can you sort out any conflicts in your life?			
Do you really listen to what others say to you?			
Do you think others really listen to you?			
Do you try to see things from other people's point of view?			
Do others try to see things from your point of view?			
Are you in charge of your own feelings or do you look to others for advice and help?			
If something doesn't go your way can you learn from what happened?			
Do you make positive decisions about your behaviour?			
Do you know when your body is giving you signals about your emotions, e.g. feeling sick/butterflies = nervous; going red/blushing = embarrassed; biting inside of mouth = worried?			
If you are unhappy can you cheer yourself up?			

© Folens (copiable page)

3.2 Who Can I Talk To?

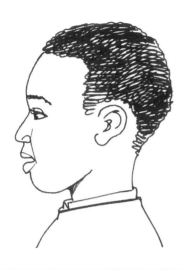

If you have a problem, are sad or need advice on something it's best to talk to someone about it. Who would you talk to and why? Use this sheet to list the top five people you would go to for help and advice. For each one say why you would go to them.

	Who?	Why?
1		
2		
3		
4		
5		

3.3 Ways Of Opening Up

Read what Zoë and Tim say about ways of opening up, managing emotions and dealing with personal pressures. Then complete the box below with the ways you open up, manage your emotions and deal with personal pressures.

This is what I do. I am very shy and when I have to talk to somebody I find it hard so I write down what I want to talk about before I meet them. I find it hard to listen to other people and get stressed in discussions so I take deep breaths and count to ten before I talk, and I always make sure what I say is relevant to the discussion. I find if I clench my fists and then unclench them it helps when I am under pressure.

I am the opposite of Zoë. I find I just gabble on and on so I decide the main points for discussion beforehand, either in my head or on paper, otherwise I would go on for ever. I know that people think I'm a know-it-all so I limit myself to a maximum of three comments in a discussion. I get too emotional and tend to get angry very quickly so I sit back in my chair and try to think calm thoughts if I do get angry, but it is difficult.

This is how I deal with things:

PLTS in PSHE: Self-Managers

© Folens (copiable page)

3.4 Can We Help?

Read the newspaper article below and then in small groups discuss questions a–c and decide on your answers. Be prepared to share your answers with the rest of the class.

Challenge Champions

When a group of Year 7 students asked a group of Year 8 students to set them a challenge to help them 'discover themselves', the Year 8 students rose to the occasion and designed the ultimate challenge – and they not only designed it they took part in it alongside the Year 7 students. The students all learned a lot about themselves and each other while doing the challenge. Chris, a Year 7 student, said 'I didn't know what I could do until I did this challenge', while Annie, a Year 8 student, said 'I learned so much about other people and what makes them tick'. So what was the challenge? It was easy – to put together an afternoon of entertainment and food for a group of 200 elderly people from the local community. Why did the Year 8 students give them that challenge? Annie says there were five reasons:

1. To give the students confidence in their own abilities.

2. To allow them to show that they could organise their time, resources and other people.

3. To show them what an amazing group of people they are.

4. To give them the confidence to perform in front of a group of people.

5. To give them the confidence to talk to a very different group of people who they would not normally talk to.

---

a What do you think the students gained from this experience?

b How does this link to the concept of 'emotional literacy'?

c What do you think would have been the main problems for the students in completing this challenge?

3.5 Being A Mentor

Briony started a new school when she was 13 and found it very difficult at first to settle in. When she was more settled she asked if she and three friends could set up a peer mentoring group called 'The Listening Ear' which would be there for students who needed someone to talk to. The group was given £250 as a start-up fund and meets three times a week after school. The group has gone from strength to strength. Briony and her friends are the first to say that it has helped them as much as it has helped the students who come to talk to them.

Now answer these questions:

a What are the rewards in being a peer mentor?

_____

_____

b What are the challenges?

_____

_____

c What are the risks?

_____

_____

d How much time do you think it takes up?

_____

_____

e How has it helped the mentors as well as the people being mentored?

_____

_____

f How does this link to 'emotional literacy'?

_____

_____

PLTS in PSHE: Self-Managers © Folens (copiable page)

Objectives

By the end of the lesson, students will:

◎ understand what it means to manage their emotions.

◎ have identified how and when to seek advice and support.

◎ have shown that they can work through challenges linked to personal problems and pressures.

Prior knowledge

None.

Links

Personal, Social, Health and Economic Education Programmes of Study for England: Personal wellbeing: 1.1 Personal identities; 1.2 Healthy lifestyles; 1.3 Risk; 1.4 Relationships.

Curriculum for Excellence for Scotland: Health and Wellbeing: Health and wellbeing: Mental, emotional, social and physical wellbeing.

Personal and Social Education Framework for Wales: Active citizenship; Health and emotional wellbeing; Moral and spiritual development.

Revised Curriculum for Northern Ireland: Learning for Life and Work: Personal understanding; Mutual understanding; Moral character.

Background

The use of peers as counsellors is now widespread in educational areas. The benefits of this approach are many and varied. Students are now trained in peer counselling and many schools have identified peer counsellors who respond to the needs and worries of other students. This unit allows students to open up those skills as well as identifying who young people can go to for advice and support. It also looks at the idea that males are less likely to seek advice and support than females and looks at the possible reasons for this.

Starter activity

Introduce a general discussion about why we all need advice and support at different times in our lives. Use some examples from current affairs/news for this as well as possible examples from your own life.

Activity sheets

Activity sheets **4.1 Can I Talk To You …? (1)** and **4.2 Can I Talk To You …? (2)** should be read through with the class and the eight problems/concerns should be discussed.

On Activity sheet **4.3 Your Advice** students should write down the advice they would give to each of the eight young people on Activity sheets **4.1** and **4.2**. It would help if this sheet was enlarged to A3 size to give more space for writing. This will give students the opportunity to give advice and support in a non-judgemental manner.

Activity sheet **4.4 Hiding Your Feelings** looks at the supposition that boys/males find it harder to talk about their feelings than girls/females do and invites students to come up with answers to this. Ideally students should not work in single sex groups for this activity – there should be at least one male and one female in each group of three. Follow this activity through by looking at the answers given and have a class vote on whether or not the supposition is actually true.

Activity sheet **4.5 Talk, Talk** encourages students to consider who to go to when they need help/advice and reinforces advice given in Unit 3 'Emotional wellbeing'. These two units could be used together as one larger unit covering two lessons.

Plenary

Students should work in pairs to talk about a time when they needed advice or support and what happened when they sought it.

Read what the young people below have to say about their worries and problems. You will also need Activity sheet 4.2.

I really worry about death and dying. My gran has just died and I keep thinking about it and what happens and if it hurts. Most of all I worry about my mum and dad dying and leaving me. I would like to talk to somebody about it all.

Caytlin

I have this problem and it worries me. I am really good at football but in the past few months I have got really angry with the other players and the ref, and I have been sent off a couple of times. I don't seem to be able to stop being angry all the time. If I don't stop it I might be thrown off the team.

Dylan

This might sound stupid but a lot of the girls in Year 10 fancy me and that worries me. I don't want to go out with any of them but they just pester me and want to talk to me and wait for me at the school gate and they send me texts. My mates say I'm lucky but I don't think I am.

Gavin

All my friends have boyfriends but I have never had one and I'm worried about that. Do you think there is something wrong with me? Will I ever get a boyfriend? I felt awful on Valentine's Day when all my mates had at least one card and I had nothing.

Sarah

Read what the young people below have to say about their worries and problems.
You will also need Activity sheet 4.1.

I worry because I am little and my mates are all a lot bigger. I have always been small but now I don't seem to be growing at all. It's terrible when we are in the showers after PE because they all laugh at me and make comments about my penis and how little it is. They say I won't be able to have sex with it.

Daniel

I hate it in maths because I can't do the work and I get really worried before the lesson. I have told my teacher about it but nothing has happened. My mum says she will come in to school to talk about it but then I'll look like an idiot. I wish I could do better in maths.

Calvin

I don't think I'll get the job I want. I really want to be a singer but everybody laughs at me and says I won't make it. I wish I could stop worrying about it but it really gets on my mind. What if it doesn't happen, I'll look stupid in front of all my mates. I have a really good voice and I am always in the school productions.

Emily

It's silly but I worry a lot about how I look and spend hours getting ready before I go out. Dad says that I'm obsessed with myself but I know that girls who don't look good get nowhere and I want to be a success so I want to look good. Everybody in music or on TV looks really fantastic so why can't I?

Anna

4.3 Your Advice!

You will need Activity sheets 4.1 and 4.2 to use with this sheet. All eight young people are suffering from pressure of some kind – some of the problems are personal, others are work- or school-related. Give each of the eight your advice on how to deal with the pressures/worries so that they can manage their emotions more effectively and, if needed, build and maintain relationships in a positive way.

Who?	My advice
1 Caytlin	
2 Dylan	
3 Gavin	
4 Sarah	
5 Daniel	
6 Calvin	
7 Emily	
8 Anna	

PLTS in PSHE: Self-Managers © Folens (copiable page)

4.4 Hiding Your Feelings

For this activity you should work in groups of three. Discuss each question and write down the answer you decide on.

a Do boys find it hard to talk about their feelings? Why?

b Are there some topics boys find it easier to talk about than others? Why?

c Do boys find it easier to talk to other males, or are they just as comfortable talking to females? Why?

4.5 Talk, Talk

Many young people find it difficult to 'open up' and talk about their worries and problems. A group of people your age have written the advice below. Read through the hints given and add your own comments about each one. Then add your own ideas and advice to help young people to open up about problems, worries and pressures.

Advice	My comments
Go to someone you like and trust, perhaps a teacher you really get on with.	
It's best to talk to friends.	
Family are good to talk to but sometimes they overreact.	
Grandparents have lots of time to listen and they always help.	
Make sure you are in a place where you feel relaxed and comfortable.	
Go to somebody who listens, not somebody who just talks about their own problems.	

My advice/ideas:

PLTS in PSHE: Self-Managers

© Folens (copiable page)

Objectives

By the end of the lesson, students will:

◎ understand what it means to be a grandparent in the twenty-first century.

◎ have identified how change can affect lives.

◎ have shown that they can organise time and resources, prioritising actions.

Prior knowledge
None.

Links

Personal, Social, Health and Economic Education Programmes of Study for England: Personal wellbeing: 1.1 Personal identities; 1.2 Healthy lifestyles; 1.3 Risk; 1.4 Relationships; 1.5 Diversity.

Curriculum for Excellence for Scotland: Health and Wellbeing: Health and wellbeing: Mental, emotional, social and physical wellbeing; Relationships, sexual health and parenthood.

Personal and Social Education Framework for Wales: Active citizenship; Health and emotional wellbeing; Moral and spiritual development.

Revised Curriculum for Northern Ireland: Learning for Life and Work: Personal understanding; Mutual understanding; Moral character; Citizenship.

Background

Many grandparents play an important role in the lives of their grandchildren. So much so that in March 2009 a report entitled 'Rethinking the family', published by the charity Grandparents Plus, called on the Government to pay grandparents for the many hours of childcare they provide for their grandchildren. The report also called for grandparents who juggle both work and care for grandchildren to receive credits towards their national insurance contributions.

Starter activity

Start a general discussion about grandparents: begin with the phrase 'a grandparent is …' and ask students to complete it.

Activity sheets

Activity sheet **5.1 What Do Grandparents Do?** asks students to consider the role of grandparents

while at the same time conducting research on grandparents within their group. The sheet allows students to organise their own time and work towards goals while showing initiative and flexibility. To encourage this we would suggest telling students initially that they have the whole lesson to complete the activity, then after 10–15 minutes reduce the time available to 40 minutes. It will be interesting to see how they cope with this change. In presenting their information to the rest of the class, students have to show initiative in their presentations and take risks as necessary.

You may have students whose grandparents have recently died. If this is the case the discussion will need delicate handling. There may be others who have never known their grandparents. You could talk about the 'ideal' grandparent if necessary.

Activity sheet **5.2 Grandparents In The News** should be read and discussed. It could then be used in conjunction with Activity sheet **5.3 Right Or Wrong?** to allow students to work in small groups to look at what changes would occur if the pay for grandparents was introduced.

Activity sheet **5.4 Golden Greats Or Groovies? (1)** allows students to enquire further into the roles of grandparents, while examining attitudes to and expectations of grandparents in general. The comments on the sheet should be read through and discussed with the concept of stereotyping introduced. Further discussion could focus on how grandparents are portrayed in the media.

Activity sheet **5.5 Golden Greats Or Groovies? (2)** should be used with Activity sheet **5.4**: students should look at the descriptions given on sheet **5.4** and write down the good/bad points for each of the grandparents described. They should then comment on any changes they would like to make to the grandparent described. Finally, students should say what kind of grandparent they would like to become.

Plenary

Discuss how students coped with the change in deadline during the lesson.

5.1 What Do Grandparents Do?

Work in small groups of three or four to complete the activities on this sheet. You have one lesson to complete all the activities. You must discuss how you are going to divide your time up to make sure that all the activities are completed, who is going to do which activity. You have five activities to complete.
These are:

a Make a list of everything a grandparent does within a 'normal' family.

b Decide how much time the 'average' grandparent spends helping out with grandchildren on a weekly basis.

c Find out about the grandparents in your group: What is their approximate age?
Do they work, and if so what job do they do? Is it full- or part-time?
What hobbies/interests do they have?

d Decide on the qualities you would look for in a grandparent and list them.

e Write up the results of these activities and present the results to the class. Will your presentation be different to the other presentations in the class – why not show initiative and make it different?

Read the newspaper article below about grandparents being paid for looking after their grandchildren.

REPORT SAYS
PAY GRANDPARENTS
FOR CHILDCARE

A recent report has called on the government to allow grandparents to receive childcare tax credit, worth up to £300 a week, if they are looking after grandchildren to help parents to work. Currently only parents who use nurseries and registered childminders can claim the money.

One in four families and half of all single parent families rely on grandparents to help with childcare every week. The value of this work is said to be around £4 billion a year.

A recent survey has found that 60 per cent of parents supported some kind of state payment to grandparents for helping to look after children.

The report also calls for 'grandparent leave' for working grandparents, to allow them to take two weeks off work following the birth of a grandchild, and to have the same rights as parents to ask for flexible working hours.

Research suggests that more and more grandparents are helping with childcare, especially in times of recession. When money is short it is grandparents who step in and help out by looking after children so that parents can go out to work or work longer hours.

LIVERPOOL JOHN MOORES UNIVERSITY
LEARNING SERVICES

5.3 Right Or Wrong?

For this activity you should work in groups of three or four. You will also need Activity sheet 5.2.

The newspaper article on Activity sheet 5.2 looks at what could be the start of a new approach to grandparents and their roles. Discuss how these changes would affect lives if they were brought in. Write down your answers in the spaces provided.

If the changes were introduced how would they affect the role of grandparents?

How would the changes affect grandparents' lives?

How would the changes affect the lives of grandchildren?

How would they affect life in general?

Overall, would the changes be for the better, or for the worse? Give reasons.

PLTS in PSHE: Self-Managers © Folens (copiable page)

5.4 Golden Greats or Groovies? (1)

What should a grandparent be like? Read what the five young people below said about their grandparents.

1 My gran and grandad are really young and my friends don't believe they are my grandparents. I call them by their first names. They wear fashionable clothes and they both work. They have a sports car and do things like sky diving for a hobby. We hardly ever see them. My dad says they are mad.

2 My nan and grandad are just what you would expect. My nan stays at home and does lots of cooking and baking and cleaning and my grandad walks the dog and fixes things in his shed. They are always there when we need them and I love going round to their house. It's so wonderful there.

3 My grandad died four years ago and my nanna has a boyfriend but we don't like to talk about it. They are really embarrassing! I suppose my nanna isn't all that old – she's 68 – but somebody her age shouldn't be doing that kind of thing. She has started going on holidays abroad and she never did that when grandad was alive. This year she went to Dubai for her birthday with her boyfriend. It feels like she isn't really ours any more.

4 They are just granny and grandad. I suppose we are lucky because they live with us in a flat above our garage and are always there for us. They are dad's mum and dad and my mum says that they 'interfere', whatever that means, but I think it's great because I can go to their flat and pig out and I can't always do that at home because mum doesn't like it.

5 He is my gramps and I love him. He takes us on adventures and we all get into trouble for getting dirty and coming back late. Gramps has lots of stories and races greyhounds and we help him. He doesn't care what he says to my dad – he says my dad is a 'twit' and we laugh when he says that. Dad doesn't laugh though.

5.5 Golden Greats Or Groovies? (2)

You will need Activity sheet 5.4 to use with this Activity sheet.

Read through the descriptions of the grandparents given on Activity sheet 5.4. For each one write down what would be the good/bad points about having that kind of grandparent and what, if anything, you would change about them and why. Then write down what kind of grandparent you would want to be, with reasons.

	Good/bad points	Changes I would make, and why
1		
2		
3		
4		
5		

If I become a grandparent this is what I would be like:

PLTS in PSHE: Self-Managers © Folens (copiable page)

Teacher's Notes

Objectives

By the end of the lesson, students will:

◎ have shown initiative and flexibility in their work.

◎ have understood the need to manage emotions and build and maintain relationships.

◎ have shown that they understand the pressures placed upon individuals.

Prior knowledge

None.

Links

Personal, Social, Health and Economic Education Programmes of Study for England: Personal wellbeing: 1.1 Personal identities; 1.3 Risk; 1.4 Relationships; 1.5 Diversity. Economic wellbeing and financial capability: 1.2 Capability; 1.3 Risk.

Curriculum for Excellence for Scotland: Health and Wellbeing: Health and wellbeing: Mental, emotional, social and physical wellbeing.

Personal and Social Education Framework for Wales: Active citizenship; Health and emotional wellbeing; Moral and spiritual development.

Revised Curriculum for Northern Ireland: Learning for Life and Work: Personal understanding; Mutual understanding; Citizenship

Background

The Civil Partnership Act 2005 came into operation on 5 December 2005. The Act enables same-sex couples to register as civil partners and thereby obtain legal recognition of their relationship. Civil partners have equal treatment to married couples in a wide range of legal matters including child support; duty to provide reasonable maintenance for your civil partner and any children of the family; ability to apply for parental responsibility for your civil partner's child.

Cryos, the world's largest sperm bank, is based in Denmark and exports sperm to 35 countries including Britain. Since 2008 (when the first children born through donor assisted conception reached 16) children born through donor assisted conception in the UK who are intending to marry can find out if they are related to their partner.

Donor assisted conception applies to both sperm and egg donation.

Starter activity

Start with a general discussion about the law regarding homosexual activity in England. It is legal from the age of 16, exactly the same as heterosexual activity. Consider why it was previously illegal between males (it has never been illegal between females) and ask students why they think the law was changed. In 1994 the law reduced the age to 18 and in 2000 it was reduced to 16.

Activity sheets

Activity sheets **6.1 Toni's Family** and **6.2 Toni's Story** introduce Toni, her problems and her 'different' family. Read through both sheets with students and discuss what they show about Toni and her family. Talk about whether or not it is a good family to be in.

Activity sheet **6.3 Fitting In?** takes statements from students at Toni's school about how she could fit in more and not be bullied. Read through this sheet with students.

Activity sheet **6.4 It's Not Right** should be used with Activity sheets **6.1**, **6.2** and **6.3**. Students have to plan a short play to help Toni by informing other students about Toni and her worries. Students should be told that they need to show initiative and flexibility in their approach to this activity and in the play they plan.

Activity sheet **6.5 What next?** uses the other four sheets in the unit. Students have a given timescale to work in and four self-management skills, behaviours and personal qualities to work towards. They must decide what happens to Toni in the five years following on from Year 11. Once students have completed this activity you should discuss their ideas with them and comment on how well they have fulfilled the four self-management skills.

Plenary

Discuss with students what, as a class and as individuals, they have learned from this activity and look at how they as individuals would respond if a friend of theirs 'came out'.

6.1 Toni's Family

My name is Toni and I am 15, nearly 16. I am in year 11 at school. I want to be a journalist and have worked hard at school to achieve good GCSE grades. I have been bullied a lot in my secondary school and I know that my family situation is the reason for this ...

Basically I have two mums and two brothers. My birth mum is Yvette and her partner is Sadie. My two brothers have Yvette as their birth mum as well and all three of us were born from the same sperm donor. Our mums have never been afraid to tell us about how we were conceived and have always been open about their relationship. Three years ago Yvette and Sadie went through a Civil Partnership which some people call a 'gay marriage'. They have been together for twenty years and are very happy. My brothers and I have never tried to hide our family set up but it has caused problems for us all. Some parents won't allow their children to come to our house and sometimes we have been asked if we are 'queer' as well. Actually, my brothers Sam and David are heterosexual and so am I which surprises some people because they automatically think we will be gay as well. School has been terrible at times and every so often I wish I came from a 'normal' family but then I say to myself – 'Hey, what's normal!' One of my friends was beaten up a lot by her dad and I think at least Yvette and Sadie love me to bits and are always there for me. Why can't people just accept us as a loving but different family instead of giving us a lot of grief? We had our windows broken a few times and even though we have lived here for ten years we do sometimes still get grief and are pointed at as being 'the only gay family in the village'.

PLTS in PSHE: Self-Managers © Folens (copiable page)

So how am I bullied? Well there are names, of course, like 'daughter of dykes', or there are references to my mums and their sexuality and people ask about whether or not they teach me 'how to be gay'. One of the worst things has always been in PE when we get changed because some of the other girls say 'Watch it!' when I'm near to them, meaning I would jump on them if I had the chance! At Christmas parties when I turn up looking feminine they make comments like 'Where's your trousers' or if I'm talking to my friends they come over and push me and say things like 'Whoops, gay alert'.

Worst of all is when I am out with my family at some village event. Everyone stops talking when we get near to them and they nudge each other and look at us. A new girl started at my school and I was asked by the Head of Year to make friends with her but when her parents heard about my family she was told not to talk to me in case 'I turned her queer'. I sometimes have sticky notes put onto my back with rude things written on them and one group of girls put nasty posters around the school saying things about me. I used to fight back and got into a lot of trouble in Years 7 and 8 but then I realised it was their problem and not mine so now I don't fight.

There are 900 students in my school and around 400 bully me but sometimes it feels like they all do. It's not only students either – some teachers find it difficult to accept my family situation and I have had comments from a couple of teachers.

6.3 Fitting In?

How could Toni fit in more and stop being bullied? Well here's our advice (we are all students at Toni's school – some of us have bullied her and some are her friends).

Just ignore everybody and show that you are not afraid of anyone. Stand tall!	Make sure your friends are all big and tough and then no one will dare to say anything to you!
Don't tell people about your family. Keep it all hidden. It's nobody else's business is it? Say that Yvette is your mum and Sadie's your aunt and when we discuss things in PSHE just keep your mouth shut.	Move to another place and start a new school, even though you are in Year 11. Move far way so that no one knows you or your family. You talk about your grandparents a lot – Yvette's parents – so go and live with them.
Get yourself a really fit boyfriend and make sure everybody knows about the two of you.	You can't stop it so get used to it. Decide what's important to you and stick to that. If you are proud of your family that's all that matters.
Go to your Head of Year and talk about it and ask if she can help stop the bullying.	Ask if it would be OK to invite your mum and Sadie in to a PSHE lesson to talk about their life. You could give your point of view as well.

PLTS in PSHE: Self-Managers © Folens (copiable page)

6.4 It's Not Right

You will need Activity sheets 6.1–6.3 to use with this Activity sheet.

Toni's friends and peers at school decided to do something to help her because the bullying was starting to affect Toni's life. They wrote and directed a short play which they performed to all year groups in assembly. The play was so successful they were asked to perform it in other secondary schools in their area. Work in small groups of three or four, imagine you are part of that group, and write down what you think should be said in the play. You need to show:

◎   initiative

◎   flexibility.

Use this sheet to decide on your title, the main roles and the main theme running through your play.

Title:

Main roles:

Main ideas/theme:

6.5 What Next?

You will need Activity sheets 6.1–6.4 to use with this Activity sheet.

Was the play a success? Did it help Toni? Were attitudes changed? What do you think happened? You have ten minutes to work out and write down what you think happened to Toni in the five years following Year 11. Discuss it in a small group of three or four and then decide what you will write down as your answer. You must:

◎ organise your time and yourselves
◎ show initiative
◎ respond to the challenge of dealing with a difficult issue
◎ manage your own emotions when dealing with this question.

When you have decided on, and written down your answer, you should discuss in your group how well you, as an individual, succeeded in meeting the four actions listed above.

This is what we think happened to Toni:

Teacher's Notes

Objectives

By the end of the lesson, students will:

◎ understand what it means to organise time and resources.

◎ have identified how they can organise themselves.

◎ have shown that they can respond to the pressures placed upon them by personal and work-related demands.

Prior knowledge

None.

Links

Personal, Social, Health and Economic Education Programmes of Study for England: Personal wellbeing: 1.1 Personal identities; 1.2 Healthy lifestyles; 1.3 Risk; 1.4 Relationships.

Curriculum for Excellence for Scotland: Health and Wellbeing: Health and wellbeing: Mental, emotional, social and physical wellbeing.

Personal and Social Education Framework for Wales: Active citizenship; Health and emotional wellbeing; Moral and spiritual development.

Revised Curriculum for Northern Ireland: Learning for Life and Work: Personal understanding; Mutual understanding; Citizenship.

Background

On 27 March 2009, the first National No Make-up Day was held. One of the reasons for the day is the fact that 'too many women spend so much time focusing on the outside – whether it's looking at glam celebs in magazines or comparing ourselves to friends – that sometimes we forget to look beneath the surface. By going without make-up for the day, women can focus on connecting with their peers emotionally rather than benchmarking them physically' (Jessica Chivers, life coach).

Starter activity

Read out the comment made by Jessica Chivers (above) and discuss it. Do students agree/disagree with its sentiments? What is the school policy regarding make-up?

Activity sheets

Activity sheets 7.1 **Make-Up Facts And Figures** and 7.2 **Make-Up And Me** should be read through and briefly discussed. Some of the students in the class could add their personal comments about make-up at this point.

Activity sheet 7.3 **Yes Or No?** should then be used with Activity sheets 7.1 and 7.2 to organise a debate on whether or not students should be allowed to wear make-up in school and whether No Make-up Day is a good or a bad idea. You should stress to students that they will have the chance to comment on how each member of their team works and that the five criteria they will be judged on are on the sheet. They should spend time discussing their views on the two related topics and write down a summary of the views along with the reasons for those views.

Activity sheet 7.4 **The Debate** should build on the work already undertaken for Activity sheet 7.3. Students should plan the debate in detail, deciding on the proposer, the seconder and the person who will give the final points. Following on from this they decide what is to be said for each of those steps. At this point you could extend the unit to another lesson by allowing the teams to actually conduct the debate and then decide who has won.

Activity sheet 7.5 **The Verdict** is for students to use to assess each person in their group on the self-managers criteria outlined on the sheet. Everyone in the group must discuss what mark should be given to each individual and have reasons for their view.

Plenary

Students should work in their groups to decide on the skills needed in a debate and whether or not they have those necessary skills. They could also look at how those skills could be of benefit in the world of work.

© Folens (copiable page)   PLTS in PSHE: Self-Managers

7.1 Make-Up Facts And Figures

1. The average female absorbs 2.3kg of chemicals through her skin every year due to make-up.

2. Some men wear make-up too: 'manscara' is mascara for men and 'guy-liner' is eyeliner for men.

3. Men are increasingly using moisturisers.

4. The male grooming market, including make-up, is worth around £750 million per year in the UK.

5. The average woman spends over £30,000 on make-up during her lifetime.

6. The average woman spends 3,276 hours putting make-up on during her lifetime – that's around two years.

7. UK women use 8,000 pints of foundation in any one year.

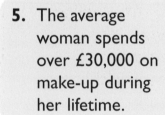

8. Over 73% of women in the UK wear some form of make-up every day.

9. National No Make-up Day was organised because it is said that females are too dependent on make-up and need to face the world without it.

© Folens (copiable page)

Read what Jenni, Sonia and Luke say about wearing make-up.

Jenni: I'm 15 and would never go out without my make-up on. I have even been suspended from school for wearing too much but I need to wear it, it gives me confidence. I grew up with make-up, I had four older sisters who wore it all the time and my mum has always worn it. By the time I was nine I was wearing lipstick and nail varnish. My dad didn't like it but he couldn't do anything about it. I feel really good about myself when I have it on. I don't wear as much as I used to when I go to school but I still wear quite a lot. It takes me around one hour to get my make-up on every morning and I am often late for school.

Sonia: As someone near to 40 I can say that I have never gone out without my full 'face' on, not since I was 14 years old. I couldn't leave the house without make-up and all my friends feel the same. I really get a buzz out of putting make-up on and I know I look great wearing it. I would hate anybody to see me without it because I know they would say 'look at the state of her'. My mum once suggested that I didn't have to wear make-up and my reply to that was 'The world is a better and more beautiful place when we wear make-up'.

Luke: I'm 26 and I am totally obsessed by my appearance. I used to borrow make-up from my sister and then my girlfriend but now I buy my own. I don't want to look like a drag queen so my make-up is subtle but I feel good when I wear it. I tend to use manscara, guy-liner, moisturiser and sometimes just a faint touch of lipstick. I have my favourite brands and have been known to spend a good hour trying out lipsticks. I'm not gay, quite the opposite, but I think if a man wants to wear make-up there's no shame in it. Famous men wear it so why shouldn't I!

7.3 Yes Or No?

Your task, using Activity sheets 7.1 and 7.2, is to organise a debate on the two following areas: whether or not students should be allowed to wear make-up in school and whether or not a 'No Make-up Day' is a good idea. Work in small groups. You MUST:

◎ organise yourselves, showing responsibility and initiative
◎ show creativity and enterprise in the way you present your argument
◎ organise your time and any possible resources
◎ prioritise your planning and actions
◎ deal with any pressures that arise.

You MUST ALSO be able to say how each person in the group dealt with the five action areas shown above.

First you must decide on what view your group will take on the two questions. Use the spaces provided below to write down your answers.

Should students be allowed to wear make-up in school? Give reasons.

Is a No Make-up Day a good idea or a bad idea? Give reasons.

PLTS in PSHE: Self-Managers © Folens (copiable page)

7.4 The Debate

You will need Activity sheet 7.3 to use with this sheet.

You have already written down your group's opinions on the two areas for debate and now you must write down what you will say in the debate. You must decide who will begin speaking and who will second the opinion and exactly what you will say. You must also decide on who will give the final points and what that person will say.

Person to give the opening points of view, i.e. the proposer:

What they will say:

Person to back up the points of view, i.e. the seconder:

What they will say:

Person to give the final points:

What they will say:

7.5 The Verdict

You must now decide how far each person in your group has worked towards the criteria which were first mentioned on Activity sheet 7.3.

You must mark each person in the group out of 10 for each of the five criteria. A score of 10 means they did as well as they possibly could, a score of 1 means they did not succeed in any way. You MUST discuss this as a group and decide as a group on the final marks.

Action areas	Name:	Score:
Organise yourselves, showing responsibility and initiative		
Show creativity and enterprise in the way you present your argument		
Organise your time and any possible resources		
Prioritise your planning and actions		
Deal with any pressures that arise		

Objectives

By the end of the lesson, students will:

◎ understand what it means to manage their emotions.

◎ have identified what the concept of a 'good life' entails.

◎ have shown that they can work through challenges linked to personal problems and pressures.

Prior knowledge

None.

Links

Personal, Social, Health and Economic Education Programmes of Study for England: Personal wellbeing: 1.1 Personal identities; 1.2 Healthy lifestyles; 1.3 Risk; 1.4 Relationships.

Curriculum for Excellence for Scotland: Health and Wellbeing: Health and wellbeing: Mental, emotional, social and physical wellbeing.

Personal and Social Education Framework for Wales: Active citizenship; Health and emotional wellbeing; Moral and spiritual development.

Revised Curriculum for Northern Ireland: Learning for Life and Work: Personal understanding; Mutual understanding.

Background

In times of economic downturn most families cut back on the amount of money they spend. However there are some families who still spend enormous amounts of money on what many other people would regard as unnecessary. Social class division is such that the Equal Opportunities Commission suggests that social difference, represented by the so called 'chav vs posh' divide, is the biggest factor affecting attainment at school. The etymology of the word 'chav' is under dispute but the most widely accepted understanding of it is that it comes from the Romany word 'chavi' meaning 'child'. In 2004 'chav' was designated by Oxford University Press as word of the year!

Starter activity

Start off a general discussion on what students understand by the word 'chav'. Look at personalities in the news who could be described as 'chavs'.

Activity sheets

Activity sheets **8.1 Rick's Life** and **8.2 Rick's Mum** should be read through and discussed. Students could consider how indicative they think the stories are of the 'chav' lifestyle.

Activity sheet **8.3 The Good Life?** should be used with Activity sheets **8.1** and **8.2**. Students are asked to consider whether or not Rick's life is 'good', and they should give reasons for their answer. They then move on to consider Rick's abilities as a self-manager, using the knowledge they have of him from Activity sheets **8.1** and **8.2**. This activity could be extended by asking students to list what they think Rick is good at.

Activity sheet **8.4 The Changes You Would Advise** should be used with Activity sheet **8.3** in order to give Rick advice about what he could do in order to be a more effective self-manager.

Activity sheet **8.5 Rick's Family** asks students to write a pen portrait for Rick, his mum and his stepdad. There are no right or wrong answers in this activity. Once students have written down their views you should discuss them as a class.

Plenary

Students should work in pairs to discuss the use of the word 'chav'. It is often used as a derogatory term referring to lower working-class people with gaudy jewellery, an ostentatious display of logos on their clothes and very lax morals. Is this correct? Do Rick and his family conform to this image?

8.1 Rick's Life

Rick is 15, almost 16. Read about his life and lifestyle.

For my sixteenth birthday my mum has promised me a customised sports car with personalised number plates, even though I won't be able to drive it until I'm seventeen. She's also going to take me on a shopping trip to New York with twenty of my mates. I already have a moped, a motorbike, a jet ski and three quad bikes so the car will be added to my collection. I can't drive any of them yet.

I have a huge en suite bedroom with everything I could want in it – three laptops, a 52-inch plasma TV, satellite system and various other things. My mum reckons she spent £52,000 on me last year but that includes clothes so it isn't as much as it sounds.

Fashion is important to me and I love diamonds so she buys me diamond earrings and rings. For my fifteenth birthday she flew me and twenty mates (different mates to the ones who will be going with me this year) to Paris and we stayed in a luxury hotel. In total that cost her £15,000 but it was great and it made her happy to spend her money on me and my mates.

When she found out she was pregnant with me she spent £30,000 on baby clothes and things for the nursery. She thinks I've got star qualities and is always trying to get me onto the TV. She says I just need to be noticed by the right people and then I'll be a star. If that doesn't happen I'd like to be a joiner; I'm already going to college two days a week for it and I'm going to have my own business like my mum. I haven't got a girlfriend, in fact I've never had one, but mum says not to worry about that.

PLTS in PSHE: Self-Managers © Folens (copiable page)

Read what Rick's mum, Annie, says about it all.

I do spoil him but he's my son and it's my money so I can do if I want! Rick has always had anything he wants and more. Spending lots of money on him gives me a real buzz. I go shopping with him every week and spend a fortune on him. My husband Harry, Rick's new stepdad, can't understand why sometimes I buy Rick twenty pairs of trousers in one go and we have arguments about it, but Rick needs to look good at all times. He has great star quality and I think he could be an international star.

My parents bought me nothing, they had no money, so what I buy Rick compensates for the fact that I had nothing at all. When I inherited all my money from my first husband I vowed that I would have a great life, and I do and so does my son. I have lots of money and I spend lots of it on him, so what! He is always very grateful for what I buy and give him and is never rude to me.

I put £1000 into his account every month for his pocket money and when he is 16 I will increase that to £2000. He needs to have his own money doesn't he? I admit I am addicted to buying things for him and the next thing will be a house for him and maybe a helicopter to get him about. That's what mums are for isn't it, to look after their children? Is he spoilt? Of course he is and I don't care who knows it. He has lots of friends and could invite two hundred friends to his party if he wanted to. Everybody wants to be his friend.

8.3 The Good Life?

Your task, using Activity sheets 8.1 and 8.2, is to decide whether or not Rick's life is 'good'. You must also assess how successful/effective Rick is in a number of given areas.

Is Rick's life 'good'? Give reasons for your opinion.

Is Rick ...	Yes/No	Reason for your opinion
able to organise himself?		
able to show personal responsibility?		
committed to learning and self-improvement?		
creative and enterprising?		
able to organise his time and resources?		
able to deal with competing pressures?		
able to manage his emotions?		
able to build and maintain relationships?		

PLTS in PSHE: Self-Managers

© Folens (copiable page)

8.4 The Changes You Would Advise

You will need Activity sheet 8.3 to use with this sheet.

On Activity sheet 8.3 you wrote down your opinions about Rick and his ability to be a self-manager. Now you must look at what you said about him and advise him on what he needs to do to improve in each area.

To **organise himself** Rick should:
To **show personal responsibility** Rick should:
To be **committed to learning and self-improvement** Rick should:
To be **creative and enterprising** Rick should:
To **organise his time and resources** Rick should:
To **deal with competing pressures** Rick should:
To **manage his emotions** Rick should:
To **build and maintain relationships** Rick should:

8.5 Rick's Family

Your task is to write a pen portrait of Rick, his mum and his stepfather using the information on Activity sheets 8.1 and 8.2.

Rick is:

Annie, his mum, is:

Harry, his stepfather, is:

Objectives

By the end of the lesson, students will:

◎ understand what it means to show personal responsibility, initiative, creativity and enterprise.
◎ understand the need to deal with competing pressures.
◎ have shown that they can organise time and resources, prioritising actions

Prior knowledge

None.

Links

Personal, Social, Health and Economic Education Programmes of Study for England: Personal wellbeing: 1.1 Personal identities; 1.3 Risk; 1.4 Relationships; 1.5 Diversity. Economic wellbeing and financial capability: 1.2 Capability; 1.3 Risk

Curriculum for Excellence for Scotland: Health and Wellbeing: Health and wellbeing: Mental, emotional, social and physical wellbeing.

Personal and Social Education Framework for Wales: Active citizenship; Health and emotional wellbeing; Moral and spiritual development.

Revised Curriculum for Northern Ireland: Learning for Life and Work: Personal understanding; Mutual understanding; Moral character.

Background

The TV series *Dragon's Den* has been adapted and used by a number of organisations as a challenge or activity to allow people to show their talents and skills. In a school setting this concept can be used to great effect for a day or as a series of lessons to enable students to work through a challenge which can have far-reaching effects on all concerned. Inviting four 'dragons' to be the judges can add an extra dimension to the work! The unit would be best completed in four lessons with one given to the introduction and to starting planning, one for the planning to be completed and one for the actual 'judging' by the 'dragons'. The fourth lesson could be given over to the feedback sheets completed by the 'dragons' and the peer assessment.

Starter activity

Show a five minute clip of the *Dragon's Den* programme and ask students to comment on it.

Activity sheets

Activity sheet **9.1 Guidance Sheet** sets out the task for students to work through. Make sure students know the criteria they will be judged on – this is shown on the sheet. Each team must identify its members and list the skills of each team member.

Activity sheet **9.2 The Product** is for students to use for their planning stage and then for final ideas. Encourage students to use their imagination and inventiveness in the creation of their product.

Activity sheet **9.3 The Presentation** should be used with Activity sheets **9.1** and **9.2** and is for students to plan what their presentation in front of the 'dragons' will be like. This page should be copied to A3 size to give more space to write on.

Activity sheet **9.4 The Feedback** is used by the 'dragons' to judge each presentation against the given criteria. All areas are to be marked out of 10 and then a final total should be calculated. The sheet will then be handed to the relevant team to look at. The team with the highest total can be judged the winners. The presentation of a suitable trophy would help with the atmosphere of this activity.

Activity sheet **9.5 Working As A Team** should be used with Activity sheet **9.4 The Feedback**. This sheet is to be used by students to assess the performance of each of their team members. The criteria given are all linked to the skills, behaviours and personal qualities outlined in the PLTS framework for 'self-managers'.

Plenary

Discuss: Why did the winning team win? What was special about them? Can each team say what they should have done in order to win?

9.1 Guidance Sheet

Have you ever watched *Dragon's Den?* Your task is to work in a team of three or four to design a product which you will then try to 'sell' to the 'dragons'. This activity is a challenge for you and will enable you to show that as a group and as individuals you can:

◎ organise yourselves
◎ show personal responsibility, initiative, creativity and enterprise
◎ show a commitment to learning and self-improvement
◎ anticipate, take and manage risks
◎ deal with pressures
◎ seek advice and support if and when needed
◎ manage your emotions and build and maintain relationships with the group.

Once you have designed your product you must present it to a team of 'dragons' who will give you feedback on your product.

Your product must be:

a   targeted at either the 14–16 or the 16–18 age group

b   under £25 to buy

c   easy to produce

d   different to anything currently on the market.

To help you get organised, write the names of your team members below and beside each name say what two skills or qualities they have.

Name	Skills/qualities

PLTS in PSHE: Self-Managers   © Folens (copiable page)

9.2 The Product

You will need Activity sheet 9.1 to help you with this activity.

Working in your teams, use this page to record your discussions and then to write down the details of the product you have decided on.

Initial ideas:

Final ideas:

Product name:

Age group:

Short description of product:

How it will be packaged:

Cost of product to the customer:

9.3 The Presentation

You will need Activity sheets 9.1 and 9.2 for this activity.

Your task here is to decide how you will give your presentation to the 'dragons'. Look back at Activity sheet 9.1 to remind yourselves of what they will be looking for: remember that this activity is not just about the product, it is also about how you appear as self-managers and you will be marked on aspects of that.

Plan what you must say during your presentation; what music, if any, you will use; what props/costumes, if any, you will use; and describe any other aspects of the presentation. You must also write down the script of what you will say, how it will be said and who will say it. Use the other side of this sheet if you need more space.

Presentation plan:

PLTS in PSHE: Self-Managers

© Folens (copiable page)

9.4 The Feedback

The panel who judged your presentation have completed this form for you as part of your feedback. Go through it and read what has been said about your product and your presentation.

All areas are marked out of 10.

Area assessed:	Comments:	Mark out of 10:
Did the team organise themselves?		
Did each member of the team show personal responsibility?		
Did the team show initiative, creativity and enterprise?		
Did the team show a commitment to learning and self-improvement?		
Did the team anticipate, take and manage risks?		
Did the team deal well with pressures?		
Did the team seek advice and support if and when needed?		
Did the team manage their emotions?		
Were relationships built and maintained within the team?		
Was the product suitable for the chosen age group?		
Was the presentation well organised?		
How well did the team deal with the demands put on them?		
Overall, how well did the team respond to the challenge?		
Overall mark		**/130**

9.5 Working As A Team

Your task is to give your personal feedback to each member of your team. Complete this sheet on your own and then, as a team, look at each sheet and read out the marks given to each other as well as any comments you wish to make.

Following the discussion, you should then complete the final statement on your own sheet.

These three columns refer to the other three members of your team. You should give each person a mark out of 10 for each area. You will not give yourself any marks!

Area	Name:	Name:	Name:
Contribution to the organisation of the team			
Was personal responsibility taken for the work?			
Was creativity shown?			
Was initiative shown?			
Was enterprise shown?			
Was there a commitment to learning and self-improvement?			
Were risks anticipated, taken and managed?			
Was pressure dealt with?			
Was advice and support looked for when it was needed?			
Were emotions managed?			
Were relationships built and maintained in the team?			
Total mark out of 110 for each person			

I agree/do not agree with my marks and comments because —————————

——————————————————————————

——————————————————————————

PLTS in PSHE: Self-Managers   © Folens (copiable page)

Objectives

By the end of the lesson, students will:

◎ have identified skills used for self-management in other areas, including in and beyond school.

◎ have reflected on the need for self-management as adults within the work place and the wider community.

◎ have worked towards goals, showing initiative, commitment and perseverance.

Prior knowledge

Awareness of self-management skills as developed through previous units.

Links

Personal, Social, Health and Economic Education Programmes of Study for England: Personal wellbeing: 1.1 Personal identities; 1.3 Risk; 1.4 Relationships.

Curriculum for Excellence for Scotland: Health and Wellbeing: Health and wellbeing: Mental, emotional, social and physical wellbeing.

Personal and Social Education Framework for Wales: Active citizenship; Health and emotional wellbeing; Preparing for lifelong learning.

Revised Curriculum for Northern Ireland: Learning for Life and Work: Personal understanding.

Background

This unit could be used after several of the previous units have been covered, as a way of making links between PSHE lessons, other areas within the school and the wider community. You could ask other teachers to highlight self-management skills within their own subjects.

Starter activity

Ask students how many of them have parents or carers who remind them to do their homework. Would they remember if they weren't reminded? Should parents remind students or should students be left to organise their own homework habits?

Activity sheets

Discuss Activity sheet **10.1 In School** to help students begin to identify examples of self-management. Ask them to match each picture with one or more of the seven skills, then suggest other examples.

Students can then take Activity sheet **10.2 Evidence** away with them and fill it in over a period of about a week to gather real life examples of when they are required to be self-managers at school. Students could compare their examples. Each student could then identify which of the seven skills they think they are weakest at, and set targets to improve in this area.

Activity sheet **10.3 Beyond School** can then be used to look at situations at home and at work.

Plenary

List resources and systems which help students become self-managers. For example, an alarm clock, diary, calendar, noticeboard at home with timetable on, to-do lists, etc. Less organised students can then think about whether or not there are any resources which might help them.

My coursework folder is finished but I've only got a 'D'. Are there any pieces I could redo which would improve my overall grade?

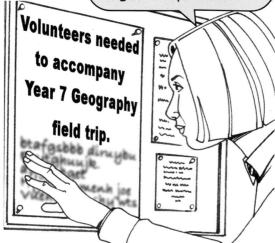

I was going to go over to Jen's this half-term but this could be good experience.

Volunteers needed to accompany Year 7 Geography field trip.

Self-management skills

◎ Seek out challenges or new responsibilities and show flexibility when priorities change.

◎ Work towards goals, showing initiative, commitment and perseverance.

◎ Organise time and resources, prioritising actions.

◎ Anticipate, take and manage risks.

◎ Deal with competing pressures, including personal and work-related demands.

◎ Respond positively to change, seeking advice and support when needed.

◎ Manage their emotions, and build and maintain relationships.

© Qualifications and Curriculum Authority

Week Begining	
Monday	
Tuesday	
Wednesday	
Thursday	
Friday	
Teacher Signature	Parent Signature

Week Begining	
Monday	
Tuesday	
Wednesday	
Thursday	
Friday	
Teacher Signature	Parent Signature

I need to start thinking about my options for Year 10.

GCSE options